# POKÉMON GO PLAY IN TRAFFIC!

# POKÉMON GO PLAY IN TRAFFIC!
## A COLORING BOOK

## STUPID DECISIONS TO COLOR & DISPLAY

BY **JABOY CALEB**    ILLUSTRATED BY **ALISSA STAPLES**

ST. MARTIN'S GRIFFIN
New York

POKÉMON GO PLAY IN TRAFFIC. Copyright © 2016 by St. Martin's Press. All rights reserved. Printed in the United States of America. For information, address St. Martin's Press, 175 Fifth Avenue, New York, N.Y. 10010. www.stmartins.com

ISBN 978-1-250-14170-5 (trade paperback)

Our books may be purchased in bulk for promotional, educational, or business use. Please contact your local bookseller or the Macmillan Corporate and Premium Sales Department at 1-800-221-7945, extension 5442, or by e-mail at MacmillanSpecialMarkets@macmillan.com.

First Edition: November 2016

10 9 8 7 6 5 4 3 2 1

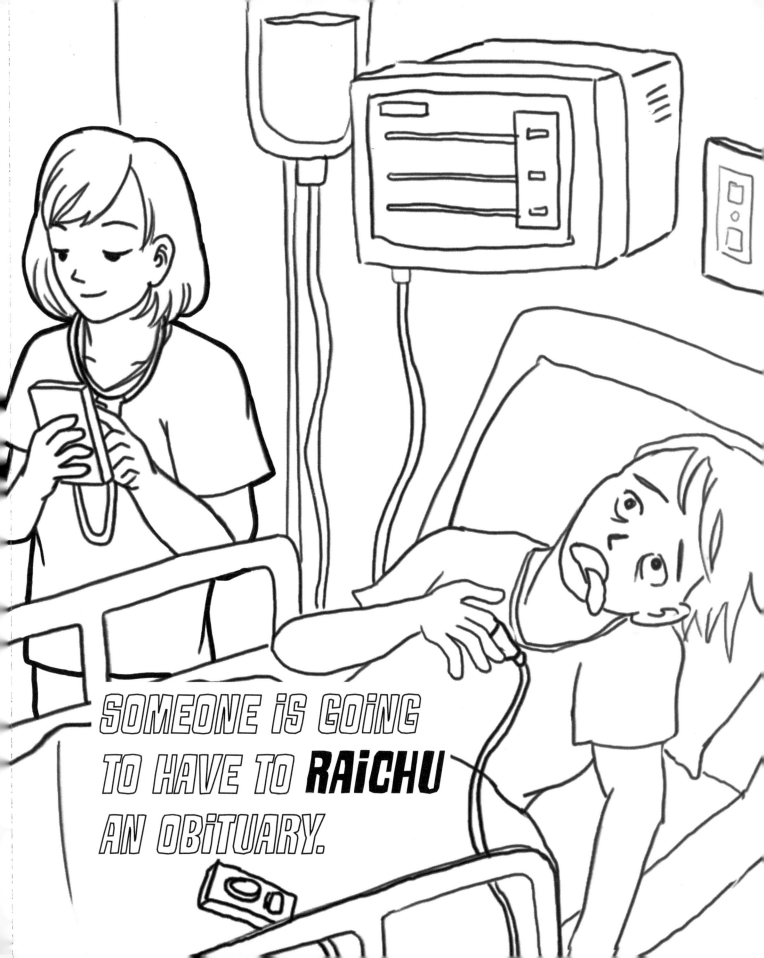

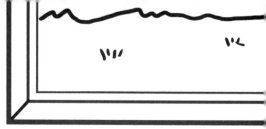
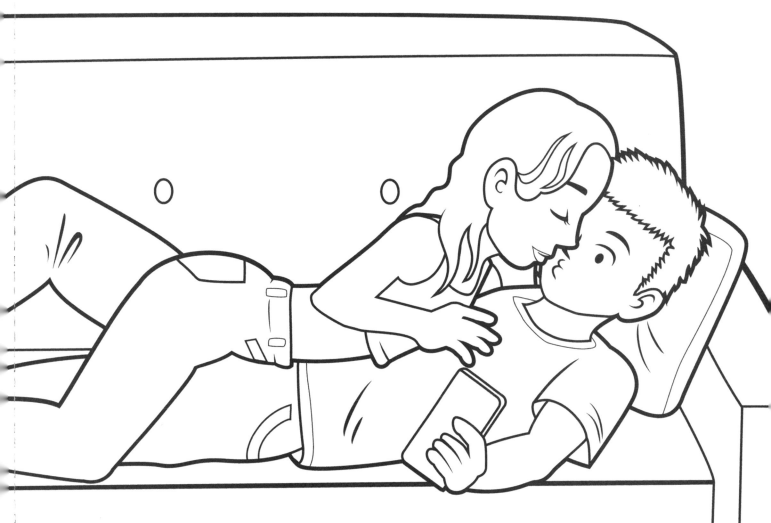

**PiKA-CHOOSE** TO DO SOMETHING BETTER WITH YOUR LIFE.

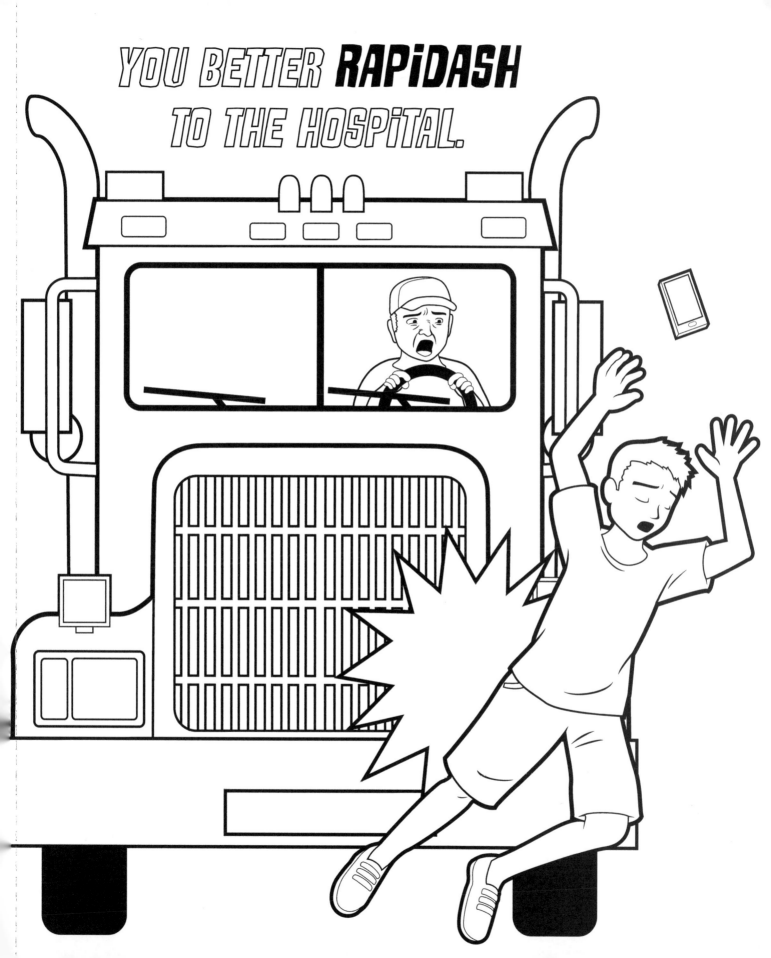

YOU SHOULD HAVE KEPT YOUR **MEOWTH** SHUT.

DANGER KEEP OUT

THIS HAS NOT BEEN A GOOD **DRAGON-NIGHT** FOR YOU.

# THIS IS A **GLOOM-Y** SITUATION.

THAT PLAN SEEMED A LITTLE BIT **FARFETCH'D**.

ARCAN'T STAND TO WATCH THIS.

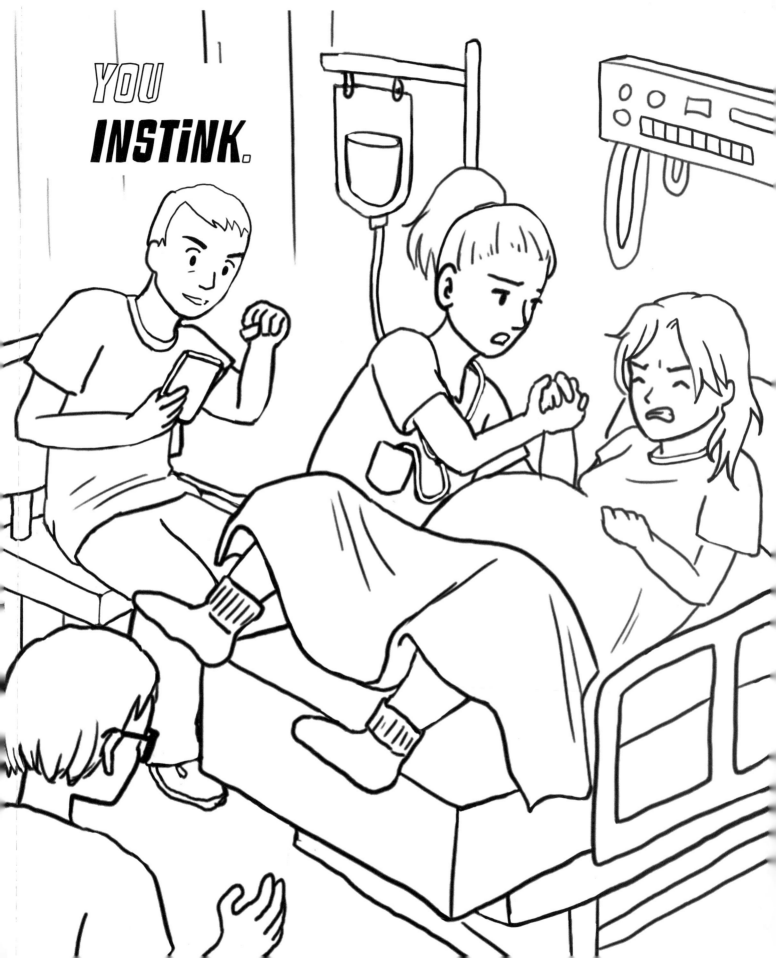

YOU ARE A **MAGNETITE** FOR DISASTER.

# DON'T TAKE ANY **CHANSEYS** WHEN IT COMES TO YOUR HEALTH.

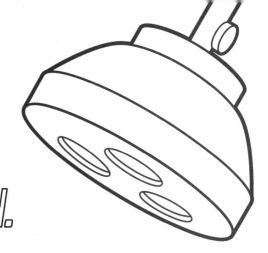

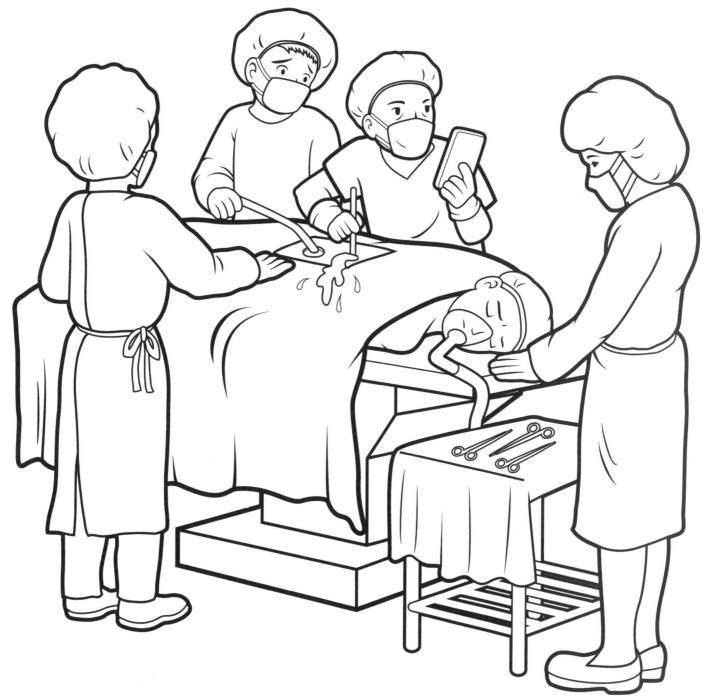

**EVEE-NTUALLY**
SOMETHING BAD IS GOING
TO HAPPEN TO YOU.